50 Cooking with Kids: Easy Recipes for Home

By: Kelly Johnson

Table of Contents

- Grilled Salmon with Lemon Butter Sauce
- Caprese Chicken Skillet
- Garlic Shrimp Linguine
- Beef Stir-Fry with Broccoli and Bell Peppers
- Creamy Mushroom Risotto
- Baked Honey Mustard Chicken
- Lemon Garlic Butter Scallops
- Spaghetti Carbonara
- Chicken Piccata with Angel Hair Pasta
- Beef Tenderloin with Red Wine Reduction
- Stuffed Bell Peppers
- Creamy Tuscan Chicken
- Shrimp Scampi with Linguine
- Pork Chops with Apple Compote
- Vegetable Stir-Fry with Tofu
- Chicken Marsala
- Seared Ahi Tuna Steaks
- Pasta Primavera
- Lemon Herb Grilled Chicken
- Baked Ziti
- Pan-Seared Ribeye Steak
- Ratatouille
- Coconut Curry Shrimp
- Spinach and Ricotta Stuffed Chicken Breast
- Mushroom and Spinach Frittata
- Garlic Butter Steak Bites
- Chicken and Broccoli Alfredo
- Teriyaki Glazed Salmon
- Pork Tenderloin with Maple Dijon Glaze
- Quinoa Stuffed Bell Peppers
- Lemon Herb Roasted Cornish Hens
- Garlic Butter Shrimp and Asparagus
- Beef and Broccoli Stir-Fry
- Creamy Pesto Pasta with Cherry Tomatoes
- Grilled Pork Skewers with Pineapple Salsa

- Baked Chicken Parmesan
- Pan-Seared Sea Bass with Mango Salsa
- Spicy Thai Basil Chicken
- Eggplant Parmesan
- Honey Garlic Glazed Salmon
- Mushroom Risotto Stuffed Bell Peppers
- Lemon Herb Grilled Lamb Chops
- Cajun Shrimp and Sausage Skillet
- Chicken and Spinach Quesadillas
- Beef Wellington with Red Wine Sauce
- Greek Lemon Chicken with Orzo
- Baked Halibut with Herbed Butter
- Stuffed Portobello Mushrooms
- Turkey Meatballs with Marinara Sauce
- Pan-Seared Scallops with Brown Butter Sauce

Grilled Salmon with Lemon Butter Sauce

Ingredients:

- 4 salmon fillets
- Salt and pepper to taste
- Olive oil, for brushing

For the lemon butter sauce:

- 1/4 cup unsalted butter
- 2 cloves garlic, minced
- Zest and juice of 1 lemon
- 2 tablespoons chopped fresh parsley
- Salt and pepper to taste

Instructions:

1. Preheat your grill to medium-high heat. Season the salmon fillets with salt and pepper on both sides.
2. Brush the grill grates with olive oil to prevent the salmon from sticking.
3. Place the seasoned salmon fillets on the grill, skin-side down. Close the grill lid and cook for about 4-5 minutes.
4. Carefully flip the salmon fillets using a spatula and cook for an additional 4-5 minutes, or until the salmon is cooked through and flakes easily with a fork.
5. While the salmon is grilling, prepare the lemon butter sauce. In a small saucepan, melt the butter over medium heat.
6. Add the minced garlic to the melted butter and cook for 1-2 minutes, until fragrant.
7. Stir in the lemon zest, lemon juice, and chopped parsley. Season with salt and pepper to taste.
8. Reduce the heat to low and let the sauce simmer for a few minutes, allowing the flavors to meld together.
9. Once the salmon is cooked, transfer it to a serving platter or individual plates. Spoon the lemon butter sauce over the grilled salmon fillets.
10. Garnish with additional chopped parsley, if desired, and serve immediately.

This grilled salmon with lemon butter sauce is perfect when served with your favorite side dishes, such as roasted vegetables, rice, or a fresh salad. It's a simple yet elegant dish that's sure to impress! Enjoy!

Caprese Chicken Skillet

Ingredients:

- 4 boneless, skinless chicken breasts
- Salt and pepper to taste
- 2 tablespoons olive oil
- 2 cloves garlic, minced
- 1 pint cherry tomatoes, halved
- 8 oz fresh mozzarella cheese, sliced
- Fresh basil leaves, chopped or torn
- Balsamic glaze or reduction, for drizzling (optional)

Instructions:

1. Season the chicken breasts with salt and pepper on both sides.
2. Heat the olive oil in a large skillet over medium-high heat. Add the chicken breasts to the skillet and cook for 5-6 minutes per side, or until they are golden brown and cooked through. Remove the chicken from the skillet and set aside on a plate.
3. In the same skillet, add the minced garlic and cherry tomatoes. Cook for 2-3 minutes, or until the tomatoes start to soften and release their juices.
4. Return the cooked chicken breasts to the skillet, placing them on top of the tomatoes.
5. Top each chicken breast with a slice of fresh mozzarella cheese.
6. Cover the skillet with a lid and cook for an additional 2-3 minutes, or until the cheese is melted and bubbly.
7. Remove the skillet from heat and garnish the Caprese chicken with chopped or torn fresh basil leaves.
8. Drizzle balsamic glaze or reduction over the chicken, if desired, for extra flavor.
9. Serve the Caprese chicken skillet immediately, with any pan juices spooned over the top.

This Caprese chicken skillet is delicious when served with a side of cooked pasta, rice, or crusty bread to soak up the flavorful sauce. It's a simple yet impressive dish that's perfect for a quick weeknight dinner or entertaining guests. Enjoy!

Garlic Shrimp Linguine

Ingredients:

- 8 oz linguine pasta
- 1 pound large shrimp, peeled and deveined
- Salt and pepper to taste
- 4 cloves garlic, minced
- 2 tablespoons olive oil
- 1/4 teaspoon red pepper flakes (optional)
- 1/4 cup white wine or chicken broth
- Juice of 1 lemon
- 2 tablespoons unsalted butter
- 2 tablespoons chopped fresh parsley
- Grated Parmesan cheese, for serving (optional)

Instructions:

1. Cook the linguine pasta according to the package instructions in a large pot of salted boiling water until al dente. Drain the pasta, reserving 1/2 cup of the pasta cooking water, and set aside.
2. Season the shrimp with salt and pepper to taste.
3. In a large skillet, heat the olive oil over medium-high heat. Add the minced garlic and red pepper flakes (if using) to the skillet and cook for 1-2 minutes, or until the garlic is fragrant.
4. Add the seasoned shrimp to the skillet and cook for 2-3 minutes per side, or until they are pink and opaque.
5. Remove the cooked shrimp from the skillet and set aside on a plate.
6. Deglaze the skillet with white wine or chicken broth, scraping up any browned bits from the bottom of the pan.
7. Add the cooked linguine pasta to the skillet along with the reserved pasta cooking water, lemon juice, and unsalted butter. Toss everything together until the pasta is well coated in the sauce.
8. Return the cooked shrimp to the skillet and toss to combine with the pasta.
9. Remove the skillet from heat and garnish the garlic shrimp linguine with chopped fresh parsley.
10. Serve the garlic shrimp linguine immediately, with grated Parmesan cheese sprinkled on top, if desired.

This garlic shrimp linguine is perfect for a quick and flavorful weeknight dinner. It's light, fresh, and bursting with garlic and lemon flavor. Enjoy!

Beef Stir-Fry with Broccoli and Bell Peppers

Ingredients:

- 1 lb flank steak or sirloin steak, thinly sliced
- 2 tablespoons soy sauce
- 1 tablespoon oyster sauce
- 1 tablespoon cornstarch
- 1 tablespoon vegetable oil
- 2 cloves garlic, minced
- 1 teaspoon grated ginger
- 1 head broccoli, cut into florets
- 2 bell peppers, thinly sliced (any color you prefer)
- Salt and pepper to taste
- Cooked rice or noodles, for serving

Instructions:

1. In a bowl, mix together the thinly sliced beef with soy sauce, oyster sauce, and cornstarch. Let it marinate for at least 15 minutes.
2. Heat the vegetable oil in a large skillet or wok over medium-high heat. Add the minced garlic and grated ginger, and cook for about 30 seconds until fragrant.
3. Add the marinated beef to the skillet in a single layer, making sure not to overcrowd the pan. Cook for 2-3 minutes without stirring, allowing the beef to sear and develop a golden brown crust.
4. Stir-fry the beef for an additional 1-2 minutes, until it is cooked through but still tender. Remove the beef from the skillet and set it aside on a plate.
5. In the same skillet, add a little more oil if needed, then add the broccoli florets and sliced bell peppers. Stir-fry for 3-4 minutes, or until the vegetables are crisp-tender.
6. Return the cooked beef to the skillet with the vegetables. Stir everything together to combine.
7. Season the beef stir-fry with salt and pepper to taste. Adjust the seasoning if necessary.
8. Serve the beef stir-fry with broccoli and bell peppers hot over cooked rice or noodles.

This beef stir-fry with broccoli and bell peppers is a delicious and nutritious meal that's packed with flavor and colorful vegetables. It's perfect for a quick weeknight dinner and can be easily customized with your favorite vegetables or sauce. Enjoy!

Creamy Mushroom Risotto

Ingredients:

- 1 1/2 cups Arborio rice
- 4 cups chicken or vegetable broth
- 2 tablespoons olive oil
- 1 onion, finely chopped
- 2 cloves garlic, minced
- 8 oz mushrooms (such as cremini or button), sliced
- 1/2 cup dry white wine
- 1/2 cup grated Parmesan cheese
- 2 tablespoons unsalted butter
- Salt and pepper to taste
- Chopped fresh parsley or thyme for garnish (optional)

Instructions:

1. In a medium saucepan, heat the chicken or vegetable broth over medium heat. Keep it warm on the stove while you prepare the risotto.
2. In a large skillet or saucepan, heat the olive oil over medium heat. Add the chopped onion and cook for 2-3 minutes, until softened.
3. Add the minced garlic to the skillet and cook for an additional 1 minute, until fragrant.
4. Add the sliced mushrooms to the skillet and cook for 5-6 minutes, stirring occasionally, until they are golden brown and tender.
5. Add the Arborio rice to the skillet and stir to coat it with the oil and vegetables. Cook for 1-2 minutes, until the rice is lightly toasted.
6. Pour the white wine into the skillet and cook, stirring constantly, until the wine is absorbed by the rice.
7. Begin adding the warm broth to the skillet, one ladleful at a time, stirring constantly and allowing each addition of broth to be absorbed before adding more. Continue this process until the rice is creamy and tender, but still slightly firm to the bite. This will take about 20-25 minutes.
8. Stir in the grated Parmesan cheese and unsalted butter until melted and creamy. Season the risotto with salt and pepper to taste.
9. Remove the skillet from heat and let the risotto rest for a minute or two.
10. Serve the creamy mushroom risotto hot, garnished with chopped fresh parsley or thyme if desired.

This creamy mushroom risotto is a luxurious and indulgent dish that's sure to impress. Serve it as a main course or as a side dish alongside roasted chicken or grilled fish. Enjoy!

Baked Honey Mustard Chicken

Ingredients:

- 4 boneless, skinless chicken breasts
- Salt and pepper to taste
- 1/3 cup Dijon mustard
- 1/4 cup honey
- 2 tablespoons olive oil
- 2 cloves garlic, minced
- 1 tablespoon soy sauce (optional)
- 1 tablespoon apple cider vinegar (optional)
- Chopped fresh parsley for garnish (optional)

Instructions:

1. Preheat your oven to 375°F (190°C). Lightly grease a baking dish with cooking spray or olive oil.
2. Season the chicken breasts with salt and pepper to taste, then arrange them in a single layer in the prepared baking dish.
3. In a small bowl, whisk together the Dijon mustard, honey, olive oil, minced garlic, soy sauce (if using), and apple cider vinegar (if using) until well combined.
4. Pour the honey mustard sauce over the chicken breasts, making sure to coat them evenly.
5. Bake the chicken in the preheated oven for 20-25 minutes, or until the chicken is cooked through and reaches an internal temperature of 165°F (75°C).
6. If desired, you can baste the chicken with the sauce halfway through baking for extra flavor and moisture.
7. Once the chicken is cooked, remove it from the oven and let it rest for a few minutes before serving.
8. Garnish the baked honey mustard chicken with chopped fresh parsley, if desired, and serve hot.

This baked honey mustard chicken pairs well with a variety of side dishes such as roasted vegetables, steamed broccoli, mashed potatoes, or a simple green salad. It's a versatile and crowd-pleasing dish that's sure to become a favorite in your household. Enjoy!

Lemon Garlic Butter Scallops

Ingredients:

- 1 pound large sea scallops
- Salt and pepper to taste
- 2 tablespoons unsalted butter
- 2 cloves garlic, minced
- Zest and juice of 1 lemon
- 2 tablespoons chopped fresh parsley
- Lemon wedges, for serving (optional)

Instructions:

1. Pat the scallops dry with paper towels, then season them generously with salt and pepper on both sides.
2. Heat a large skillet over medium-high heat. Add the butter to the skillet and let it melt.
3. Once the butter is melted and hot, add the minced garlic to the skillet. Cook for about 30 seconds, until the garlic is fragrant but not browned.
4. Carefully add the scallops to the skillet in a single layer, making sure not to overcrowd the pan. Cook the scallops for 2-3 minutes on one side, until they develop a golden brown crust.
5. Flip the scallops over and cook for an additional 2-3 minutes on the other side, until they are opaque and cooked through.
6. Add the lemon zest and lemon juice to the skillet, stirring gently to coat the scallops with the lemon garlic butter sauce.
7. Sprinkle the chopped fresh parsley over the scallops, then remove the skillet from heat.
8. Serve the lemon garlic butter scallops immediately, garnished with lemon wedges if desired.

These lemon garlic butter scallops are delicious when served with rice, pasta, or crusty bread to soak up the flavorful sauce. They're perfect for a romantic dinner at home or any special occasion. Enjoy!

Spaghetti Carbonara

Ingredients:

- 12 oz spaghetti
- 4 oz pancetta or bacon, diced
- 3 cloves garlic, minced
- 2 large eggs
- 1 cup grated Parmesan cheese, plus extra for serving
- 1/4 cup chopped fresh parsley
- Salt and black pepper to taste

Instructions:

1. Cook the spaghetti in a large pot of salted boiling water according to the package instructions until al dente. Reserve 1 cup of pasta water, then drain the spaghetti and set aside.
2. While the spaghetti is cooking, heat a large skillet over medium heat. Add the diced pancetta or bacon to the skillet and cook until crispy and golden brown, about 5-7 minutes.
3. Add the minced garlic to the skillet with the cooked pancetta or bacon and cook for an additional 1-2 minutes, until fragrant.
4. In a separate bowl, whisk together the eggs, grated Parmesan cheese, and chopped parsley until well combined.
5. Once the spaghetti is cooked and drained, immediately add it to the skillet with the pancetta or bacon and garlic. Toss everything together over low heat until the spaghetti is well coated in the pancetta fat.
6. Remove the skillet from heat and quickly pour the egg and cheese mixture over the hot spaghetti, stirring vigorously to coat the pasta evenly. The residual heat from the spaghetti will cook the eggs and create a creamy sauce.
7. If the carbonara seems too thick, you can add a splash of reserved pasta water to loosen it up.
8. Season the spaghetti carbonara with salt and black pepper to taste.
9. Serve the spaghetti carbonara immediately, garnished with extra grated Parmesan cheese and chopped parsley if desired.

Spaghetti carbonara is best enjoyed fresh and hot, so serve it immediately after preparing. It's a simple yet indulgent dish that's perfect for a cozy dinner at home or a special occasion. Enjoy!

Chicken Piccata with Angel Hair Pasta

Ingredients:

For the chicken:

- 4 boneless, skinless chicken breasts
- Salt and pepper to taste
- 1/2 cup all-purpose flour
- 2 tablespoons olive oil
- 4 tablespoons unsalted butter
- 1/2 cup chicken broth
- 1/4 cup fresh lemon juice
- 1/4 cup capers, drained
- 1/4 cup chopped fresh parsley (optional)
- Lemon slices for garnish (optional)

For the angel hair pasta:

- 8 oz angel hair pasta
- Salt for pasta water
- 2 tablespoons olive oil
- 2 cloves garlic, minced
- 1/4 cup chopped fresh parsley
- Salt and pepper to taste
- Grated Parmesan cheese for serving (optional)

Instructions:

1. Prepare the chicken: Place each chicken breast between two sheets of plastic wrap and pound them to an even thickness using a meat mallet or rolling pin. Season both sides of the chicken breasts with salt and pepper.
2. Dredge the chicken breasts in flour, shaking off any excess.
3. Heat the olive oil and 2 tablespoons of butter in a large skillet over medium-high heat. Add the chicken breasts to the skillet and cook for 3-4 minutes on each side, or until they are golden brown and cooked through. Remove the chicken from the skillet and set aside on a plate.
4. In the same skillet, add the chicken broth, lemon juice, and capers. Bring the mixture to a simmer, scraping up any browned bits from the bottom of the skillet.

5. Return the chicken breasts to the skillet and simmer for an additional 2-3 minutes, allowing the flavors to meld together. Stir in the chopped parsley, if using.
6. Meanwhile, prepare the angel hair pasta according to the package instructions in a large pot of salted boiling water until al dente. Drain the pasta, reserving 1/2 cup of pasta water.
7. In a separate skillet, heat the olive oil over medium heat. Add the minced garlic and cook for 1-2 minutes, until fragrant.
8. Add the cooked angel hair pasta to the skillet with the garlic, along with the chopped parsley. Toss everything together until the pasta is well coated in the garlic-infused oil. If the pasta seems dry, you can add a splash of reserved pasta water to loosen it up.
9. Season the pasta with salt and pepper to taste.
10. Serve the chicken piccata over the angel hair pasta, spooning the lemon caper sauce over the top. Garnish with lemon slices and grated Parmesan cheese, if desired.

Chicken piccata with angel hair pasta is a delicious and satisfying meal that's sure to impress. It's perfect for a romantic dinner at home or any special occasion. Enjoy!

Beef Tenderloin with Red Wine Reduction

Ingredients:

- 2 lbs beef tenderloin, trimmed and tied
- Salt and pepper to taste
- 2 tablespoons olive oil
- 4 cloves garlic, minced
- 1 shallot, finely chopped
- 1 cup red wine (such as Cabernet Sauvignon or Merlot)
- 1 cup beef broth
- 2 tablespoons balsamic vinegar
- 2 tablespoons unsalted butter
- Fresh thyme sprigs for garnish (optional)

Instructions:

1. Preheat your oven to 400°F (200°C). Season the beef tenderloin generously with salt and pepper on all sides.
2. Heat the olive oil in a large oven-safe skillet over medium-high heat. Add the beef tenderloin to the skillet and sear it on all sides until it is browned, about 2-3 minutes per side.
3. Transfer the skillet to the preheated oven and roast the beef tenderloin for 15-20 minutes, or until it reaches your desired level of doneness. Use a meat thermometer inserted into the thickest part of the tenderloin to check for doneness (125°F for medium-rare, 135°F for medium). Remove the skillet from the oven and transfer the beef tenderloin to a cutting board to rest.
4. While the beef tenderloin is resting, place the skillet back on the stovetop over medium heat. Add the minced garlic and chopped shallot to the skillet and cook for 1-2 minutes, until softened.
5. Pour the red wine into the skillet and use a wooden spoon to scrape up any browned bits from the bottom of the skillet. Simmer the wine for 5-7 minutes, or until it has reduced by half.
6. Add the beef broth and balsamic vinegar to the skillet and continue to simmer for another 5-7 minutes, until the sauce has thickened slightly.
7. Remove the skillet from heat and whisk in the unsalted butter until it is melted and the sauce is smooth. Season the sauce with salt and pepper to taste.
8. Slice the beef tenderloin into thick slices and arrange them on a serving platter. Pour the red wine reduction sauce over the beef tenderloin slices.

9. Garnish the beef tenderloin with fresh thyme sprigs, if desired, and serve immediately.

Beef tenderloin with red wine reduction is a decadent and elegant dish that's sure to impress your guests. Serve it with your favorite side dishes such as mashed potatoes, roasted vegetables, or a green salad for a complete meal. Enjoy!

Stuffed Bell Peppers

Ingredients:

- 4 large bell peppers, any color
- 1 lb ground beef or turkey
- 1 small onion, finely chopped
- 2 cloves garlic, minced
- 1 cup cooked rice (white or brown)
- 1 cup tomato sauce
- 1 teaspoon dried oregano
- 1 teaspoon dried basil
- Salt and pepper to taste
- 1 cup shredded cheese (such as cheddar or mozzarella)
- Fresh parsley or basil for garnish (optional)

Instructions:

1. Preheat your oven to 375°F (190°C). Grease a baking dish large enough to hold the bell peppers.
2. Cut the tops off the bell peppers and remove the seeds and membranes from inside. You can slice a thin layer off the bottom of each pepper if they don't stand up straight.
3. In a skillet over medium heat, cook the ground beef or turkey until browned. Add the chopped onion and garlic, and cook until the onion is softened.
4. Stir in the cooked rice, tomato sauce, dried oregano, dried basil, salt, and pepper. Cook for an additional 2-3 minutes, until heated through.
5. Spoon the filling mixture into the hollowed-out bell peppers, packing it down firmly.
6. Place the stuffed bell peppers upright in the prepared baking dish. If you have any leftover filling, you can spoon it around the peppers.
7. Cover the baking dish with aluminum foil and bake the stuffed bell peppers in the preheated oven for 30 minutes.
8. Remove the foil from the baking dish and sprinkle the shredded cheese over the tops of the stuffed bell peppers.
9. Return the baking dish to the oven and bake for an additional 10-15 minutes, or until the cheese is melted and bubbly.
10. Remove the stuffed bell peppers from the oven and let them cool slightly before serving.

11. Garnish the stuffed bell peppers with fresh parsley or basil, if desired, and serve hot.

Stuffed bell peppers are a hearty and satisfying meal that's perfect for a family dinner or entertaining guests. Feel free to customize the filling with your favorite ingredients such as beans, quinoa, or different types of cheese. Enjoy!

Creamy Tuscan Chicken

Ingredients:

- 4 boneless, skinless chicken breasts
- Salt and pepper to taste
- 2 tablespoons olive oil
- 4 cloves garlic, minced
- 1/2 cup sun-dried tomatoes, drained and chopped
- 1 cup chicken broth
- 1 cup heavy cream
- 1 teaspoon dried Italian seasoning
- 2 cups fresh baby spinach
- 1/2 cup grated Parmesan cheese
- Fresh parsley for garnish (optional)

Instructions:

1. Season the chicken breasts with salt and pepper on both sides.
2. Heat the olive oil in a large skillet over medium-high heat. Add the chicken breasts to the skillet and cook for 5-6 minutes on each side, or until they are golden brown and cooked through. Remove the chicken from the skillet and set aside on a plate.
3. In the same skillet, add the minced garlic and chopped sun-dried tomatoes. Cook for 1-2 minutes, until the garlic is fragrant.
4. Pour the chicken broth into the skillet, using a wooden spoon to scrape up any browned bits from the bottom of the pan.
5. Stir in the heavy cream and dried Italian seasoning. Bring the mixture to a simmer and let it cook for 5 minutes, until slightly thickened.
6. Add the fresh baby spinach to the skillet and cook for 1-2 minutes, until wilted.
7. Stir in the grated Parmesan cheese until melted and creamy.
8. Return the cooked chicken breasts to the skillet and spoon the creamy Tuscan sauce over the top.
9. Let the chicken simmer in the sauce for a few minutes to heat through.
10. Garnish the creamy Tuscan chicken with fresh parsley, if desired, and serve hot.

Creamy Tuscan chicken is delicious when served over cooked pasta, rice, or mashed potatoes. It's a comforting and flavorful dish that's perfect for a cozy dinner at home. Enjoy!

Shrimp Scampi with Linguine

Ingredients:

- 12 oz linguine pasta
- 1 lb large shrimp, peeled and deveined
- Salt and pepper to taste
- 4 tablespoons unsalted butter
- 4 cloves garlic, minced
- 1/4 teaspoon red pepper flakes (optional)
- 1/4 cup white wine or chicken broth
- Juice of 1 lemon
- 2 tablespoons chopped fresh parsley
- Grated Parmesan cheese for serving (optional)

Instructions:

1. Cook the linguine pasta according to the package instructions in a large pot of salted boiling water until al dente. Drain the pasta and set aside, reserving 1/2 cup of pasta water.
2. While the pasta is cooking, season the shrimp with salt and pepper to taste.
3. In a large skillet, melt the butter over medium heat. Add the minced garlic and red pepper flakes (if using) to the skillet and cook for 1-2 minutes, until the garlic is fragrant.
4. Add the seasoned shrimp to the skillet and cook for 2-3 minutes per side, or until they are pink and opaque. Remove the shrimp from the skillet and set aside on a plate.
5. Deglaze the skillet with white wine or chicken broth, scraping up any browned bits from the bottom of the pan.
6. Add the cooked linguine pasta to the skillet along with the reserved pasta water and lemon juice. Toss everything together until the pasta is well coated in the sauce.
7. Return the cooked shrimp to the skillet and toss to combine with the pasta.
8. Stir in the chopped fresh parsley and season with additional salt and pepper to taste.
9. Serve the shrimp scampi with linguine immediately, garnished with grated Parmesan cheese if desired.

Shrimp scampi with linguine is delicious when served with a side of crusty bread or a simple green salad. It's a quick and flavorful dish that's perfect for a weeknight dinner or special occasion. Enjoy!

Pork Chops with Apple Compote

Ingredients:

For the pork chops:

- 4 bone-in pork chops, about 3/4 inch thick
- Salt and pepper to taste
- 2 tablespoons olive oil

For the apple compote:

- 2 large apples, peeled, cored, and diced (such as Granny Smith or Honeycrisp)
- 2 tablespoons unsalted butter
- 2 tablespoons brown sugar
- 1/2 teaspoon ground cinnamon
- Pinch of ground nutmeg
- Pinch of salt
- 1/4 cup apple cider or apple juice
- 1 tablespoon lemon juice

Instructions:

1. Preheat your oven to 375°F (190°C).
2. Season the pork chops generously with salt and pepper on both sides.
3. Heat the olive oil in a large oven-safe skillet over medium-high heat. Add the pork chops to the skillet and sear them for 2-3 minutes on each side, until they are browned.
4. Transfer the skillet to the preheated oven and roast the pork chops for 10-15 minutes, or until they reach an internal temperature of 145°F (63°C) for medium doneness. Remove the skillet from the oven and transfer the pork chops to a plate to rest.
5. While the pork chops are roasting, prepare the apple compote. In a saucepan, melt the butter over medium heat. Add the diced apples, brown sugar, cinnamon, nutmeg, and salt to the saucepan. Cook, stirring occasionally, for 5-7 minutes, until the apples are softened.
6. Stir in the apple cider or apple juice and lemon juice. Simmer the mixture for an additional 5 minutes, until the liquid has reduced slightly and the apples are tender.

7. Serve the pork chops hot, topped with the warm apple compote.
8. Garnish the pork chops with additional chopped fresh herbs such as parsley or thyme, if desired.

Pork chops with apple compote are delicious when served with mashed potatoes, roasted vegetables, or a side of green beans. It's a comforting and flavorful dish that's perfect for a cozy dinner at home. Enjoy!

Vegetable Stir-Fry with Tofu

Ingredients:

- 14 oz block of firm tofu, drained and pressed
- 2 tablespoons soy sauce
- 1 tablespoon rice vinegar
- 1 tablespoon sesame oil
- 1 tablespoon cornstarch
- 2 tablespoons vegetable oil
- 2 cloves garlic, minced
- 1 tablespoon minced ginger
- 1 onion, thinly sliced
- 2 bell peppers, thinly sliced (any color you prefer)
- 2 carrots, julienned or thinly sliced
- 1 cup broccoli florets
- 1 cup snow peas, trimmed
- Salt and pepper to taste
- Cooked rice or noodles, for serving

For the sauce:

- 1/4 cup soy sauce
- 2 tablespoons hoisin sauce
- 1 tablespoon rice vinegar
- 1 tablespoon brown sugar
- 1 teaspoon sesame oil
- 1 teaspoon cornstarch dissolved in 2 tablespoons water

Instructions:

1. Start by preparing the tofu. Cut the tofu into cubes and place them in a bowl. In a separate small bowl, mix together 2 tablespoons of soy sauce, 1 tablespoon of rice vinegar, 1 tablespoon of sesame oil, and 1 tablespoon of cornstarch. Pour this marinade over the tofu cubes and gently toss to coat. Let the tofu marinate for at least 15 minutes.
2. In a small bowl, whisk together all the ingredients for the sauce: 1/4 cup soy sauce, 2 tablespoons hoisin sauce, 1 tablespoon rice vinegar, 1 tablespoon

brown sugar, 1 teaspoon sesame oil, and the cornstarch dissolved in water. Set the sauce aside.
3. Heat 1 tablespoon of vegetable oil in a large skillet or wok over medium-high heat. Add the marinated tofu cubes to the skillet in a single layer and cook for 2-3 minutes on each side, or until they are golden brown and crispy. Remove the tofu from the skillet and set aside on a plate.
4. In the same skillet, add another tablespoon of vegetable oil. Add the minced garlic and minced ginger to the skillet and cook for 1-2 minutes, until fragrant.
5. Add the sliced onion, bell peppers, carrots, broccoli florets, and snow peas to the skillet. Stir-fry the vegetables for 5-6 minutes, or until they are crisp-tender.
6. Return the cooked tofu to the skillet with the vegetables. Pour the sauce over the tofu and vegetables, stirring gently to coat everything evenly. Cook for an additional 1-2 minutes, until the sauce has thickened slightly.
7. Season the vegetable stir-fry with salt and pepper to taste.
8. Serve the vegetable stir-fry with tofu hot over cooked rice or noodles.

Vegetable stir-fry with tofu is a delicious and healthy dish that's packed with flavor and nutrients. Feel free to customize the vegetables according to your preferences or what you have on hand. Enjoy!

Chicken Marsala

Ingredients:

- 4 boneless, skinless chicken breasts
- Salt and pepper to taste
- 1/2 cup all-purpose flour, for dredging
- 4 tablespoons unsalted butter
- 2 tablespoons olive oil
- 8 oz mushrooms, sliced
- 2 cloves garlic, minced
- 1 cup Marsala wine
- 1 cup chicken broth
- 2 tablespoons chopped fresh parsley, for garnish (optional)

Instructions:

1. Season the chicken breasts with salt and pepper on both sides. Dredge the chicken breasts in flour, shaking off any excess.
2. In a large skillet, heat 2 tablespoons of butter and 1 tablespoon of olive oil over medium-high heat. Add the chicken breasts to the skillet and cook for 4-5 minutes on each side, or until they are golden brown and cooked through. Remove the chicken from the skillet and set aside on a plate.
3. In the same skillet, add the remaining butter and olive oil. Add the sliced mushrooms to the skillet and cook for 5-6 minutes, or until they are golden brown and tender. Add the minced garlic to the skillet and cook for an additional minute, until fragrant.
4. Pour the Marsala wine into the skillet, using a wooden spoon to scrape up any browned bits from the bottom of the pan. Allow the wine to simmer for 2-3 minutes, until it has reduced slightly.
5. Stir in the chicken broth and bring the mixture to a simmer. Let it cook for another 5 minutes, until the sauce has thickened slightly.
6. Return the cooked chicken breasts to the skillet, spooning the sauce and mushrooms over the top. Let the chicken simmer in the sauce for a few minutes to heat through.
7. Garnish the Chicken Marsala with chopped fresh parsley, if desired, and serve hot.

Chicken Marsala is delicious when served with mashed potatoes, pasta, or crusty bread to soak up the flavorful sauce. It's a comforting and elegant dish that's perfect for a special dinner at home. Enjoy!

Seared Ahi Tuna Steaks

Ingredients:

- 2 ahi tuna steaks, about 6-8 ounces each
- Salt and pepper to taste
- 1 tablespoon sesame seeds (optional)
- 1 tablespoon vegetable oil or sesame oil
- Soy sauce, for serving
- Wasabi paste, for serving
- Pickled ginger, for serving
- Sliced green onions, for garnish (optional)
- Lemon wedges, for serving

Instructions:

1. Pat the ahi tuna steaks dry with paper towels and season them generously with salt and pepper on both sides. If using sesame seeds, sprinkle them over both sides of the tuna steaks and press gently to adhere.
2. Heat the vegetable oil or sesame oil in a skillet over high heat until it's very hot. You want the skillet to be smoking hot to get a good sear on the tuna.
3. Carefully place the tuna steaks in the hot skillet and sear them for about 1-2 minutes on each side, depending on the thickness of the steaks and how rare you prefer them. For medium-rare, aim for about 1 minute per side. You want the outside to be nicely seared while the inside remains pink.
4. Once the tuna steaks are seared to your liking, remove them from the skillet and transfer them to a cutting board. Let them rest for a few minutes before slicing.
5. Slice the seared ahi tuna steaks thinly against the grain.
6. Serve the sliced tuna steaks immediately, drizzled with soy sauce and wasabi paste on the side for dipping. Garnish with pickled ginger, sliced green onions, and lemon wedges if desired.

Seared ahi tuna steaks are delicious when served with steamed rice, Asian-style noodles, or a fresh salad. Enjoy this restaurant-quality dish in the comfort of your own home!

Pasta Primavera

Ingredients:

- 8 oz pasta (such as spaghetti, fettuccine, or penne)
- 2 tablespoons olive oil
- 2 cloves garlic, minced
- 1 small onion, thinly sliced
- 1 bell pepper, thinly sliced (any color you prefer)
- 1 cup cherry tomatoes, halved
- 1 cup broccoli florets
- 1 cup sliced mushrooms
- 1 cup fresh spinach leaves
- Salt and pepper to taste
- Grated Parmesan cheese for serving (optional)
- Chopped fresh herbs (such as basil or parsley) for garnish (optional)

Instructions:

1. Cook the pasta according to the package instructions in a large pot of salted boiling water until al dente. Drain the pasta and set aside.
2. While the pasta is cooking, heat the olive oil in a large skillet over medium heat. Add the minced garlic and thinly sliced onion to the skillet and cook for 2-3 minutes, until softened.
3. Add the sliced bell pepper, halved cherry tomatoes, broccoli florets, and sliced mushrooms to the skillet. Cook, stirring occasionally, for 5-6 minutes, or until the vegetables are tender-crisp.
4. Add the cooked pasta and fresh spinach leaves to the skillet with the vegetables. Toss everything together until the pasta is well coated and the spinach is wilted.
5. Season the pasta primavera with salt and pepper to taste.
6. Serve the pasta primavera hot, garnished with grated Parmesan cheese and chopped fresh herbs if desired.

Pasta primavera is a versatile dish, so feel free to customize it with your favorite spring vegetables or whatever you have on hand. You can also add cooked chicken, shrimp, or tofu for extra protein if desired. Enjoy this delicious and colorful pasta dish as a light and satisfying meal!

Lemon Herb Grilled Chicken

Ingredients:

- 4 boneless, skinless chicken breasts
- Zest and juice of 1 lemon
- 2 tablespoons olive oil
- 2 cloves garlic, minced
- 1 tablespoon chopped fresh herbs (such as rosemary, thyme, or oregano)
- Salt and pepper to taste
- Lemon wedges, for serving
- Chopped fresh parsley or additional herbs for garnish (optional)

Instructions:

1. In a small bowl, whisk together the lemon zest, lemon juice, olive oil, minced garlic, chopped fresh herbs, salt, and pepper to make the marinade.
2. Place the chicken breasts in a shallow dish or a large resealable plastic bag. Pour the marinade over the chicken, making sure it's evenly coated. Cover the dish or seal the bag, then refrigerate and let the chicken marinate for at least 30 minutes, or up to 4 hours for maximum flavor.
3. Preheat your grill to medium-high heat. If you're using a charcoal grill, make sure the coals are evenly distributed and glowing orange.
4. Remove the chicken from the marinade and discard any excess marinade.
5. Place the chicken breasts on the preheated grill and cook for 6-8 minutes per side, or until they are cooked through and no longer pink in the center. The internal temperature of the chicken should reach 165°F (75°C) when measured with a meat thermometer.
6. Once the chicken is cooked, remove it from the grill and let it rest for a few minutes before serving.
7. Serve the lemon herb grilled chicken hot, garnished with lemon wedges and chopped fresh parsley or additional herbs if desired.

Lemon herb grilled chicken pairs well with a variety of side dishes, such as grilled vegetables, rice, or a fresh salad. It's a simple yet flavorful dish that's sure to be a hit at your next barbecue or dinner party. Enjoy!

Baked Ziti

Ingredients:

- 12 oz ziti pasta
- 1 tablespoon olive oil
- 1 onion, finely chopped
- 2 cloves garlic, minced
- 1 lb ground beef or Italian sausage
- 1 (24 oz) jar of marinara sauce
- 1 teaspoon dried oregano
- 1 teaspoon dried basil
- Salt and pepper to taste
- 1 cup ricotta cheese
- 1 cup shredded mozzarella cheese
- 1/2 cup grated Parmesan cheese
- Chopped fresh parsley for garnish (optional)

Instructions:

1. Preheat your oven to 375°F (190°C). Grease a 9x13-inch baking dish and set aside.
2. Cook the ziti pasta according to the package instructions in a large pot of salted boiling water until al dente. Drain the pasta and set aside.
3. In a large skillet, heat the olive oil over medium heat. Add the chopped onion and minced garlic to the skillet and cook for 2-3 minutes, until softened.
4. Add the ground beef or Italian sausage to the skillet and cook, breaking it up with a spoon, until browned and cooked through.
5. Stir in the marinara sauce, dried oregano, dried basil, salt, and pepper. Simmer the sauce for 5-7 minutes, allowing the flavors to meld together.
6. In a large bowl, combine the cooked ziti pasta with the sauce mixture, ricotta cheese, and half of the shredded mozzarella and grated Parmesan cheese. Mix until everything is well combined.
7. Transfer the pasta mixture to the prepared baking dish and spread it out evenly. Sprinkle the remaining shredded mozzarella and grated Parmesan cheese over the top.
8. Cover the baking dish with aluminum foil and bake the baked ziti in the preheated oven for 20 minutes.

9. Remove the foil from the baking dish and continue baking the ziti for an additional 10 minutes, or until the cheese is melted and bubbly.
10. Remove the baked ziti from the oven and let it cool for a few minutes before serving. Garnish with chopped fresh parsley, if desired.

Baked ziti is delicious served hot with a side of garlic bread and a green salad. It's a hearty and comforting dish that's sure to be a hit with the whole family. Enjoy!

Pan-Seared Ribeye Steak

Ingredients:

- 2 ribeye steaks, about 1 inch thick
- Salt and pepper to taste
- 2 tablespoons vegetable oil or clarified butter (ghee)

Instructions:

1. Remove the ribeye steaks from the refrigerator and let them sit at room temperature for about 30 minutes. This allows the steaks to cook more evenly.
2. Pat the steaks dry with paper towels and season them generously with salt and pepper on both sides.
3. Heat a large skillet (preferably cast iron) over medium-high heat. Add the vegetable oil or clarified butter to the skillet and heat until it's shimmering but not smoking.
4. Carefully place the ribeye steaks in the hot skillet. Make sure there is enough space between the steaks to allow for even cooking.
5. Cook the steaks for 3-4 minutes on the first side without moving them. This allows a nice sear to develop.
6. Flip the steaks using a pair of tongs and cook for an additional 3-4 minutes on the other side, or until they reach your desired level of doneness. For medium-rare, the internal temperature should be around 130-135°F (55-57°C) when measured with a meat thermometer inserted into the thickest part of the steak.
7. Once the steaks are cooked to your liking, remove them from the skillet and transfer them to a cutting board. Let the steaks rest for 5-10 minutes before slicing.
8. Slice the ribeye steaks against the grain into thick slices and serve immediately.

Pan-seared ribeye steak pairs well with a variety of side dishes such as mashed potatoes, roasted vegetables, or a simple green salad. Enjoy this delicious and satisfying dish!

Ratatouille

Ingredients:

- 1 large eggplant, diced
- 2 zucchini, diced
- 2 yellow squash, diced
- 1 onion, diced
- 2 bell peppers (red, yellow, or orange), diced
- 4 cloves garlic, minced
- 2 cups diced tomatoes (fresh or canned)
- 2 tablespoons tomato paste
- 2 teaspoons dried herbs de Provence (or a mixture of dried thyme, rosemary, oregano, and basil)
- Salt and pepper to taste
- Olive oil for cooking
- Chopped fresh parsley or basil for garnish (optional)

Instructions:

1. Heat a few tablespoons of olive oil in a large pot or Dutch oven over medium heat. Add the diced eggplant to the pot and cook, stirring occasionally, for about 5 minutes, or until it starts to soften.
2. Add the diced zucchini, yellow squash, onion, and bell peppers to the pot. Cook, stirring occasionally, for another 5 minutes, or until the vegetables are slightly softened.
3. Add the minced garlic to the pot and cook for 1-2 minutes, until fragrant.
4. Stir in the diced tomatoes, tomato paste, and dried herbs de Provence. Season the ratatouille with salt and pepper to taste.
5. Reduce the heat to low and let the ratatouille simmer gently for 20-30 minutes, stirring occasionally, until all the vegetables are tender and the flavors have melded together.
6. Taste and adjust the seasoning if needed.
7. Serve the ratatouille hot, garnished with chopped fresh parsley or basil if desired.

Ratatouille is delicious served on its own as a vegetarian main course or as a side dish alongside grilled meat or fish. It can also be enjoyed cold or at room temperature. This versatile dish is perfect for using up summer vegetables and is sure to be a hit with family and friends. Enjoy!

Coconut Curry Shrimp

Ingredients:

- 1 lb shrimp, peeled and deveined
- 2 tablespoons coconut oil or vegetable oil
- 1 onion, finely chopped
- 3 cloves garlic, minced
- 1 tablespoon grated ginger
- 2 tablespoons curry powder
- 1 teaspoon ground turmeric
- 1 can (13.5 oz) coconut milk
- 1 cup chicken or vegetable broth
- 1 tablespoon fish sauce (optional)
- 1 tablespoon brown sugar or honey (optional)
- Salt and pepper to taste
- Fresh cilantro or chopped green onions for garnish
- Cooked rice or naan bread for serving

Instructions:

1. Heat the coconut oil or vegetable oil in a large skillet or wok over medium heat. Add the chopped onion and cook for 2-3 minutes until softened.
2. Add the minced garlic and grated ginger to the skillet and cook for another minute until fragrant.
3. Stir in the curry powder and ground turmeric and cook for an additional minute to toast the spices.
4. Add the shrimp to the skillet and cook for 2-3 minutes until they start to turn pink.
5. Pour in the coconut milk and chicken or vegetable broth. Stir in the fish sauce and brown sugar or honey if using. Season with salt and pepper to taste.
6. Bring the mixture to a simmer and cook for 5-7 minutes until the shrimp are cooked through and the sauce has thickened slightly.
7. Taste and adjust the seasoning if needed.
8. Serve the coconut curry shrimp hot over cooked rice or with naan bread for dipping. Garnish with fresh cilantro or chopped green onions.

Coconut curry shrimp is delicious and aromatic, with a perfect balance of sweetness and spice. It's a versatile dish that can be customized with your favorite vegetables or additional protein. Enjoy!

Spinach and Ricotta Stuffed Chicken Breast

Ingredients:

- 4 boneless, skinless chicken breasts
- Salt and pepper to taste
- 1 cup ricotta cheese
- 1 cup chopped fresh spinach
- 1/2 cup shredded mozzarella cheese
- 2 cloves garlic, minced
- 1/4 cup grated Parmesan cheese
- 1 teaspoon dried Italian seasoning
- Olive oil for cooking
- Toothpicks or kitchen twine

Instructions:

1. Preheat your oven to 375°F (190°C).
2. Use a sharp knife to butterfly each chicken breast: lay the breast flat on a cutting board, and with your hand flat on top of it, carefully slice horizontally into the thickest part of the breast, stopping about 1/2 inch from the edge so you can open it like a book.
3. Season the inside of each butterflied chicken breast with salt and pepper to taste.
4. In a mixing bowl, combine the ricotta cheese, chopped spinach, shredded mozzarella cheese, minced garlic, grated Parmesan cheese, and dried Italian seasoning. Mix well to combine.
5. Spoon the spinach and ricotta mixture evenly onto one half of each butterflied chicken breast. Fold the other half over the filling to close it, and secure with toothpicks or kitchen twine.
6. Heat some olive oil in a large oven-safe skillet over medium-high heat. Once the oil is hot, add the stuffed chicken breasts to the skillet and cook for 3-4 minutes on each side, until they are golden brown.
7. Transfer the skillet to the preheated oven and bake the stuffed chicken breasts for 20-25 minutes, or until they are cooked through and the internal temperature reaches 165°F (75°C).
8. Remove the skillet from the oven and let the stuffed chicken breasts rest for a few minutes before serving.

9. Serve the spinach and ricotta stuffed chicken breasts hot, garnished with additional grated Parmesan cheese and chopped fresh parsley if desired.

Spinach and ricotta stuffed chicken breast is delicious when served with a side of pasta, roasted vegetables, or a fresh salad. It's a flavorful and impressive dish that's sure to impress your family and friends. Enjoy!

Mushroom and Spinach Frittata

Ingredients:

- 8 large eggs
- 1/4 cup milk or cream
- Salt and pepper to taste
- 2 tablespoons olive oil
- 1 small onion, finely chopped
- 8 oz mushrooms, sliced
- 2 cups fresh spinach leaves, chopped
- 1/2 cup shredded cheese (such as cheddar, mozzarella, or Swiss)
- Fresh herbs (such as parsley or chives) for garnish (optional)

Instructions:

1. Preheat your oven to 350°F (175°C).
2. In a large bowl, whisk together the eggs, milk or cream, salt, and pepper until well combined. Set aside.
3. Heat the olive oil in a large oven-safe skillet over medium heat. Add the chopped onion to the skillet and cook for 2-3 minutes until softened.
4. Add the sliced mushrooms to the skillet and cook for another 5-6 minutes, stirring occasionally, until they are golden brown and any liquid has evaporated.
5. Add the chopped spinach to the skillet and cook for 1-2 minutes until wilted.
6. Pour the egg mixture over the mushrooms and spinach in the skillet. Stir gently to distribute the ingredients evenly.
7. Cook the frittata on the stovetop for 3-4 minutes, until the edges are set but the center is still slightly runny.
8. Sprinkle the shredded cheese evenly over the top of the frittata.
9. Transfer the skillet to the preheated oven and bake the frittata for 10-12 minutes, or until the center is set and the top is golden brown.
10. Remove the skillet from the oven and let the frittata cool for a few minutes before slicing.
11. Garnish the mushroom and spinach frittata with fresh herbs if desired, then slice and serve.

Mushroom and spinach frittata can be served hot, warm, or at room temperature. It's delicious on its own or paired with a side salad, crusty bread, or roasted potatoes. Enjoy this flavorful and satisfying dish any time of day!

Garlic Butter Steak Bites

Ingredients:

- 1 lb steak (such as sirloin, flank, or ribeye), cut into bite-sized pieces
- Salt and pepper to taste
- 2 tablespoons butter
- 4 cloves garlic, minced
- 1 tablespoon chopped fresh parsley (optional)
- Lemon wedges for serving (optional)

Instructions:

1. Season the bite-sized steak pieces with salt and pepper to taste.
2. Heat a large skillet over medium-high heat. Add the butter to the skillet and let it melt.
3. Once the butter is melted and hot, add the minced garlic to the skillet. Cook for about 1 minute, stirring constantly, until the garlic is fragrant but not browned.
4. Add the seasoned steak pieces to the skillet in a single layer. Let them cook without stirring for 1-2 minutes to allow a nice sear to develop on one side.
5. Use tongs to flip the steak pieces and cook for an additional 1-2 minutes, or until they are browned on all sides and cooked to your desired level of doneness. Keep in mind that cooking time will vary depending on the thickness of the steak pieces and your preferred level of doneness.
6. Once the steak bites are cooked to your liking, remove the skillet from the heat.
7. Sprinkle the chopped fresh parsley over the steak bites, if using, and toss to coat.
8. Serve the garlic butter steak bites hot, garnished with lemon wedges if desired.

Garlic butter steak bites are delicious served on their own as an appetizer or main course, or served over pasta, rice, or mashed potatoes for a more substantial meal. They're quick and easy to make, and sure to be a hit with family and friends. Enjoy!

Chicken and Broccoli Alfredo

Ingredients:

- 8 oz fettuccine or any pasta of your choice
- 2 boneless, skinless chicken breasts, cut into bite-sized pieces
- Salt and pepper to taste
- 2 tablespoons olive oil
- 2 cloves garlic, minced
- 2 cups broccoli florets
- 1 cup heavy cream
- 1/2 cup grated Parmesan cheese
- 1/4 cup chopped fresh parsley (optional)
- Lemon zest (optional)

Instructions:

1. Cook the pasta according to the package instructions in a large pot of salted boiling water until al dente. Drain the pasta and set aside.
2. Season the chicken breast pieces with salt and pepper to taste.
3. Heat the olive oil in a large skillet over medium-high heat. Add the seasoned chicken breast pieces to the skillet and cook for 5-6 minutes, or until they are golden brown and cooked through. Remove the chicken from the skillet and set aside.
4. In the same skillet, add the minced garlic and cook for 1-2 minutes, until fragrant.
5. Add the broccoli florets to the skillet and cook for 3-4 minutes, or until they are tender-crisp.
6. Reduce the heat to medium-low and pour the heavy cream into the skillet. Stir in the grated Parmesan cheese and cook, stirring occasionally, until the sauce is heated through and slightly thickened.
7. Return the cooked chicken breast pieces to the skillet and toss to coat them in the Alfredo sauce.
8. Add the cooked pasta to the skillet and toss everything together until the pasta is well coated in the sauce.
9. Garnish the chicken and broccoli Alfredo with chopped fresh parsley and lemon zest, if desired.

Chicken and broccoli Alfredo is delicious served hot, garnished with extra Parmesan cheese and cracked black pepper if desired. Enjoy this creamy and comforting pasta dish for a satisfying meal!

Teriyaki Glazed Salmon

Ingredients:

- 4 salmon fillets (about 6 oz each), skin-on or skinless
- Salt and pepper to taste
- 1/4 cup soy sauce
- 2 tablespoons honey or maple syrup
- 1 tablespoon rice vinegar
- 1 tablespoon sesame oil
- 2 cloves garlic, minced
- 1 teaspoon grated ginger
- 1 tablespoon cornstarch (optional, for thickening the sauce)
- 2 tablespoons water (optional, for thinning the sauce)
- Sesame seeds and sliced green onions for garnish (optional)

Instructions:

1. Preheat your oven to 400°F (200°C).
2. Season the salmon fillets with salt and pepper to taste and place them on a baking sheet lined with parchment paper or aluminum foil.
3. In a small bowl, whisk together the soy sauce, honey or maple syrup, rice vinegar, sesame oil, minced garlic, and grated ginger to make the teriyaki sauce.
4. Pour half of the teriyaki sauce over the salmon fillets, reserving the remaining sauce for later.
5. Bake the salmon in the preheated oven for 12-15 minutes, or until the salmon is cooked through and flakes easily with a fork. Cooking time will vary depending on the thickness of your salmon fillets.
6. While the salmon is baking, you can thicken the reserved teriyaki sauce, if desired. In a small saucepan, whisk together the cornstarch and water until smooth. Add the reserved teriyaki sauce to the saucepan and bring it to a simmer over medium heat. Cook for 2-3 minutes, stirring constantly, until the sauce has thickened. Remove from heat.
7. Once the salmon is cooked, remove it from the oven and brush it with the thickened teriyaki sauce.
8. Serve the teriyaki glazed salmon hot, garnished with sesame seeds and sliced green onions if desired. Enjoy!

Teriyaki glazed salmon pairs well with steamed rice and your favorite vegetables for a complete and satisfying meal. It's a simple and delicious dish that's sure to become a family favorite!

Pork Tenderloin with Maple Dijon Glaze

Ingredients:

For the pork tenderloin:

- 1 pork tenderloin (about 1 to 1.5 pounds)
- Salt and pepper to taste
- 1 tablespoon olive oil

For the maple Dijon glaze:

- 1/4 cup maple syrup
- 2 tablespoons Dijon mustard
- 1 tablespoon soy sauce
- 1 tablespoon apple cider vinegar
- 2 cloves garlic, minced
- 1 teaspoon dried thyme (or 1 tablespoon fresh thyme leaves)
- Salt and pepper to taste

Instructions:

1. Preheat your oven to 400°F (200°C).
2. Season the pork tenderloin generously with salt and pepper on all sides.
3. In a small bowl, whisk together the maple syrup, Dijon mustard, soy sauce, apple cider vinegar, minced garlic, and dried thyme until well combined.
4. Heat olive oil in an ovenproof skillet over medium-high heat. Once the skillet is hot, add the pork tenderloin and sear it on all sides until it's golden brown, about 2-3 minutes per side.
5. Remove the skillet from the heat and brush the maple Dijon glaze all over the pork tenderloin, reserving some glaze for later.
6. Transfer the skillet to the preheated oven and roast the pork tenderloin for about 15-20 minutes, or until it reaches an internal temperature of 145°F (63°C) for medium doneness. Baste the pork tenderloin with the reserved glaze halfway through the cooking time.
7. Once cooked, remove the skillet from the oven and tent the pork tenderloin with foil. Let it rest for about 5-10 minutes before slicing.

8. Slice the pork tenderloin into thick slices and serve it with any remaining maple Dijon glaze drizzled over the top.
9. Garnish with fresh thyme leaves or chopped parsley, if desired.

Pork tenderloin with maple Dijon glaze pairs wonderfully with roasted vegetables, mashed potatoes, or a side of steamed greens. Enjoy this delicious and flavorful dish!

Quinoa Stuffed Bell Peppers

Ingredients:

- 4 large bell peppers (any color), halved and seeds removed
- 1 cup quinoa, rinsed
- 2 cups vegetable broth or water
- 1 tablespoon olive oil
- 1 onion, diced
- 2 cloves garlic, minced
- 1 carrot, diced
- 1 zucchini, diced
- 1 cup diced tomatoes (fresh or canned)
- 1 teaspoon ground cumin
- 1 teaspoon paprika
- Salt and pepper to taste
- 1/2 cup shredded cheese (such as cheddar or mozzarella)
- Fresh parsley or cilantro for garnish (optional)

Instructions:

1. Preheat your oven to 375°F (190°C). Arrange the halved bell peppers in a baking dish, cut side up, and set aside.
2. In a medium saucepan, combine the quinoa and vegetable broth (or water). Bring to a boil, then reduce the heat to low, cover, and simmer for 15-20 minutes, or until the quinoa is cooked and the liquid is absorbed. Remove from heat and set aside.
3. In a large skillet, heat the olive oil over medium heat. Add the diced onion and cook for 2-3 minutes, until softened.
4. Add the minced garlic, diced carrot, and diced zucchini to the skillet. Cook for another 3-4 minutes, until the vegetables are tender.
5. Stir in the diced tomatoes, ground cumin, paprika, salt, and pepper. Cook for 2-3 minutes, allowing the flavors to meld together.
6. Add the cooked quinoa to the skillet with the vegetable mixture and stir to combine.
7. Spoon the quinoa and vegetable mixture evenly into each bell pepper half, pressing down gently to pack it in.
8. Sprinkle the shredded cheese over the top of each stuffed bell pepper half.

9. Cover the baking dish with aluminum foil and bake in the preheated oven for 25-30 minutes, or until the bell peppers are tender and the cheese is melted and bubbly.
10. Remove the foil from the baking dish and bake for an additional 5 minutes, or until the cheese is golden brown.
11. Remove from the oven and let the stuffed bell peppers cool slightly before serving.
12. Garnish with fresh parsley or cilantro, if desired, and serve hot.

Quinoa stuffed bell peppers are delicious on their own or served with a side salad for a complete meal. They're perfect for meal prep and can be enjoyed for lunch or dinner throughout the week. Enjoy!

Lemon Herb Roasted Cornish Hens

Ingredients:

- 2 Cornish hens, about 1 to 1.5 pounds each
- Salt and pepper to taste
- 2 tablespoons olive oil
- 2 cloves garlic, minced
- Zest of 1 lemon
- Juice of 1 lemon
- 1 tablespoon chopped fresh herbs (such as rosemary, thyme, and parsley)
- Lemon slices for garnish
- Fresh herbs for garnish

Instructions:

1. Preheat your oven to 375°F (190°C).
2. Pat the Cornish hens dry with paper towels. Season the hens generously with salt and pepper, both inside and out.
3. In a small bowl, mix together the olive oil, minced garlic, lemon zest, lemon juice, and chopped fresh herbs to make the herb marinade.
4. Rub the herb marinade all over the Cornish hens, ensuring they are coated evenly.
5. Place the Cornish hens in a roasting pan or baking dish, breast-side up.
6. Roast the Cornish hens in the preheated oven for 50-60 minutes or until the internal temperature reaches 165°F (75°C) when measured with a meat thermometer inserted into the thickest part of the thigh.
7. Baste the Cornish hens with the pan juices occasionally during the cooking process to keep them moist.
8. Once cooked, remove the Cornish hens from the oven and let them rest for a few minutes.
9. Garnish the roasted Cornish hens with lemon slices and fresh herbs before serving.
10. Serve the lemon herb roasted Cornish hens hot, accompanied by your favorite side dishes like roasted vegetables or mashed potatoes.

These lemon herb roasted Cornish hens are flavorful, tender, and make for an impressive meal. Enjoy the wonderful aroma and taste of these beautifully roasted hens!

Garlic Butter Shrimp and Asparagus

Ingredients:

- 1 lb large shrimp, peeled and deveined
- 1 lb asparagus, ends trimmed and cut into bite-sized pieces
- 4 tablespoons unsalted butter
- 4 cloves garlic, minced
- Salt and pepper to taste
- 1 tablespoon lemon juice
- 1 tablespoon chopped fresh parsley (optional)
- Lemon wedges for serving (optional)

Instructions:

1. Heat 2 tablespoons of butter in a large skillet over medium-high heat.
2. Add the minced garlic to the skillet and cook for about 30 seconds, until fragrant.
3. Add the shrimp to the skillet and season with salt and pepper to taste. Cook the shrimp for 2-3 minutes on each side, or until they are pink and opaque. Remove the shrimp from the skillet and set aside.
4. In the same skillet, add the remaining 2 tablespoons of butter. Add the asparagus to the skillet and season with salt and pepper to taste. Cook the asparagus for 4-5 minutes, or until they are tender-crisp.
5. Return the cooked shrimp to the skillet with the asparagus. Add the lemon juice and chopped parsley (if using), and toss everything together to coat evenly.
6. Cook for an additional minute to heat everything through.
7. Remove the skillet from the heat and serve the garlic butter shrimp and asparagus hot, garnished with lemon wedges if desired.

Garlic butter shrimp and asparagus pairs well with rice, pasta, or crusty bread. It's a delicious and satisfying dish that's perfect for a quick weeknight dinner or a special occasion. Enjoy!

Beef and Broccoli Stir-Fry

Ingredients:

- 1 lb flank steak or sirloin, thinly sliced against the grain
- 2 tablespoons soy sauce
- 1 tablespoon rice wine or dry sherry
- 1 tablespoon cornstarch
- 2 tablespoons vegetable oil, divided
- 3 cloves garlic, minced
- 1 teaspoon grated ginger
- 1 head broccoli, cut into florets
- 1/2 cup beef broth or water
- 2 tablespoons oyster sauce
- 1 tablespoon hoisin sauce (optional)
- Salt and pepper to taste
- Cooked rice for serving

Instructions:

1. In a bowl, combine the sliced beef with soy sauce, rice wine (or dry sherry), and cornstarch. Mix well to coat the beef evenly. Let it marinate for 15-20 minutes.
2. Heat 1 tablespoon of vegetable oil in a large skillet or wok over high heat. Add the marinated beef to the skillet in a single layer and cook for 1-2 minutes on each side, or until browned. Remove the beef from the skillet and set aside.
3. In the same skillet, add the remaining tablespoon of vegetable oil. Add the minced garlic and grated ginger to the skillet and cook for about 30 seconds, until fragrant.
4. Add the broccoli florets to the skillet and stir-fry for 3-4 minutes, or until they are tender-crisp.
5. Return the cooked beef to the skillet with the broccoli.
6. In a small bowl, mix together the beef broth (or water), oyster sauce, and hoisin sauce (if using). Pour the sauce mixture over the beef and broccoli in the skillet.
7. Stir-fry everything together for an additional 1-2 minutes, until the sauce has thickened slightly and everything is heated through.
8. Season with salt and pepper to taste.
9. Remove the skillet from the heat and serve the beef and broccoli stir-fry hot, with cooked rice on the side.

Beef and broccoli stir-fry is a delicious and satisfying dish that's perfect for a quick weeknight dinner. Enjoy!

Creamy Pesto Pasta with Cherry Tomatoes

Ingredients:

- 8 oz pasta (such as spaghetti, fettuccine, or penne)
- 1 cup cherry tomatoes, halved
- 2 tablespoons olive oil
- 2 cloves garlic, minced
- 1/2 cup heavy cream
- 1/4 cup pesto sauce (homemade or store-bought)
- Salt and pepper to taste
- Grated Parmesan cheese for serving (optional)
- Fresh basil leaves for garnish (optional)

Instructions:

1. Cook the pasta according to the package instructions in a large pot of salted boiling water until al dente. Drain the pasta, reserving 1/2 cup of the pasta cooking water.
2. While the pasta is cooking, heat the olive oil in a large skillet over medium heat. Add the minced garlic to the skillet and cook for 1-2 minutes, until fragrant.
3. Add the halved cherry tomatoes to the skillet and cook for 3-4 minutes, until they start to soften and release their juices.
4. Stir in the heavy cream and pesto sauce, and bring the mixture to a simmer. Cook for 2-3 minutes, stirring occasionally, until the sauce is heated through and slightly thickened.
5. Add the cooked pasta to the skillet with the creamy pesto sauce and cherry tomatoes. Toss everything together until the pasta is well coated in the sauce. If the sauce is too thick, you can add some of the reserved pasta cooking water to thin it out.
6. Season the creamy pesto pasta with salt and pepper to taste.
7. Remove the skillet from the heat and serve the pasta hot, garnished with grated Parmesan cheese and fresh basil leaves if desired.

Creamy pesto pasta with cherry tomatoes is delicious on its own or served with a side salad or garlic bread. It's a simple yet flavorful dish that's sure to become a favorite!

Grilled Pork Skewers with Pineapple Salsa

Ingredients:

For the pork skewers:

- 1 lb pork tenderloin or pork loin, cut into cubes
- 2 tablespoons olive oil
- 2 cloves garlic, minced
- 1 teaspoon paprika
- 1 teaspoon ground cumin
- 1 teaspoon ground coriander
- Salt and pepper to taste
- Bamboo skewers, soaked in water for 30 minutes

For the pineapple salsa:

- 2 cups fresh pineapple, diced
- 1/2 red bell pepper, diced
- 1/4 red onion, finely chopped
- 1 jalapeño pepper, seeded and minced
- 1/4 cup chopped fresh cilantro
- Juice of 1 lime
- Salt and pepper to taste

Instructions:

1. In a bowl, combine the olive oil, minced garlic, paprika, ground cumin, ground coriander, salt, and pepper. Add the cubed pork to the bowl and toss to coat evenly. Let the pork marinate for at least 30 minutes, or up to 2 hours in the refrigerator.
2. While the pork is marinating, prepare the pineapple salsa. In a separate bowl, combine the diced pineapple, diced red bell pepper, finely chopped red onion, minced jalapeño pepper, chopped fresh cilantro, lime juice, salt, and pepper. Stir well to combine. Cover and refrigerate until ready to use.
3. Preheat your grill to medium-high heat.

4. Thread the marinated pork cubes onto the soaked bamboo skewers, dividing them evenly among the skewers.
5. Place the pork skewers on the preheated grill and cook for 8-10 minutes, turning occasionally, until the pork is cooked through and nicely browned on all sides.
6. Remove the pork skewers from the grill and let them rest for a few minutes.
7. Serve the grilled pork skewers hot, accompanied by the pineapple salsa on the side.

Grilled pork skewers with pineapple salsa are delicious served with rice, quinoa, or couscous, and a side of grilled vegetables. Enjoy this flavorful and tropical dish at your next barbecue or summer gathering!

Baked Chicken Parmesan

Ingredients:

For the chicken:

- 4 boneless, skinless chicken breasts
- Salt and pepper to taste
- 1 cup all-purpose flour
- 2 large eggs, beaten
- 1 cup breadcrumbs (plain or seasoned)
- 1/2 cup grated Parmesan cheese
- 1 teaspoon dried oregano
- 1 teaspoon dried basil
- 1/2 teaspoon garlic powder
- Cooking spray or olive oil, for greasing

For assembly:

- 2 cups marinara sauce
- 1 cup shredded mozzarella cheese
- Fresh basil leaves, chopped (optional)
- Cooked spaghetti or pasta, for serving (optional)

Instructions:

1. Preheat your oven to 400°F (200°C). Grease a baking dish with cooking spray or olive oil.
2. Season the chicken breasts with salt and pepper on both sides.
3. Set up a breading station with three shallow bowls: one with flour, one with beaten eggs, and one with breadcrumbs mixed with grated Parmesan cheese, dried oregano, dried basil, and garlic powder.
4. Dredge each chicken breast in the flour, shaking off any excess. Dip it into the beaten eggs, allowing any excess to drip off. Then coat it in the breadcrumb mixture, pressing gently to adhere.
5. Place the breaded chicken breasts in the prepared baking dish. If desired, you can drizzle a little olive oil over the top of each chicken breast to help them crisp up in the oven.

6. Bake the chicken in the preheated oven for 20-25 minutes, or until the chicken is cooked through and the coating is golden brown and crispy.
7. Remove the baking dish from the oven and spoon marinara sauce evenly over each chicken breast. Sprinkle shredded mozzarella cheese over the top.
8. Return the baking dish to the oven and bake for an additional 5-10 minutes, or until the cheese is melted and bubbly.
9. Garnish the baked chicken parmesan with chopped fresh basil leaves, if desired.
10. Serve the baked chicken parmesan hot, with cooked spaghetti or pasta on the side if desired.

Baked chicken parmesan is delicious served with a side salad, garlic bread, or roasted vegetables. It's a comforting and satisfying meal that's sure to please the whole family!

Pan-Seared Sea Bass with Mango Salsa

Ingredients:

For the sea bass:

- 4 sea bass fillets, skin-on or skinless
- Salt and pepper to taste
- 2 tablespoons olive oil
- 2 tablespoons butter
- 2 cloves garlic, minced
- 1 teaspoon paprika
- 1/2 teaspoon dried thyme or fresh thyme leaves

For the mango salsa:

- 1 ripe mango, peeled, pitted, and diced
- 1/2 red bell pepper, diced
- 1/4 red onion, finely chopped
- 1 jalapeño pepper, seeded and minced
- Juice of 1 lime
- 2 tablespoons chopped fresh cilantro
- Salt and pepper to taste

Instructions:

1. Start by preparing the mango salsa. In a bowl, combine the diced mango, diced red bell pepper, finely chopped red onion, minced jalapeño pepper, lime juice, chopped fresh cilantro, salt, and pepper. Stir well to combine. Cover and refrigerate until ready to use.
2. Season the sea bass fillets with salt, pepper, and paprika on both sides.
3. Heat the olive oil and butter in a large skillet over medium-high heat. Once the skillet is hot, add the minced garlic and dried thyme (or fresh thyme leaves) to the skillet and cook for about 1 minute, until fragrant.
4. Carefully place the seasoned sea bass fillets in the skillet, skin-side down if they have skin. Cook for 3-4 minutes on one side without moving them, until the bottom is nicely browned and crispy.

5. Carefully flip the sea bass fillets using a spatula and cook for an additional 3-4 minutes on the other side, or until the fish is cooked through and flakes easily with a fork. The cooking time will depend on the thickness of your fish fillets.
6. Once the sea bass is cooked, remove the skillet from the heat.
7. Serve the pan-seared sea bass hot, topped with the mango salsa on top or on the side.
8. Garnish with additional chopped cilantro and lime wedges if desired.

Pan-seared sea bass with mango salsa is delicious served with rice, quinoa, or couscous, and a side of steamed vegetables. Enjoy this light and flavorful dish for a refreshing meal!

Spicy Thai Basil Chicken

Ingredients:

- 500g chicken breast or thigh, thinly sliced
- 2 tablespoons vegetable oil
- 4 cloves garlic, minced
- 4-6 Thai bird's eye chilies, chopped (adjust to taste)
- 1 red bell pepper, sliced
- 1 onion, sliced
- 1 cup fresh basil leaves, loosely packed
- 2 tablespoons soy sauce
- 1 tablespoon oyster sauce
- 1 tablespoon fish sauce
- 1 teaspoon sugar
- Cooked rice, for serving

Instructions:

1. Prepare Ingredients: Thinly slice the chicken breast or thigh. Mince the garlic and chop the Thai bird's eye chilies. Slice the red bell pepper and onion. Pick the basil leaves from the stems and set aside.
2. Heat Oil: Heat vegetable oil in a large skillet or wok over medium-high heat.
3. Sauté Aromatics: Add minced garlic and chopped Thai bird's eye chilies to the hot oil. Sauté for about 30 seconds or until fragrant.
4. Cook Chicken: Add the sliced chicken to the skillet. Stir-fry until the chicken is cooked through, about 5-7 minutes.
5. Add Vegetables: Once the chicken is cooked, add the sliced red bell pepper and onion to the skillet. Stir-fry for an additional 2-3 minutes until the vegetables are tender but still crisp.
6. Season: In a small bowl, mix together soy sauce, oyster sauce, fish sauce, and sugar. Pour this sauce mixture over the chicken and vegetables. Stir well to combine.
7. Add Basil: Add the fresh basil leaves to the skillet. Stir-fry for another minute until the basil leaves wilt and release their aroma.
8. Serve: Remove from heat. Serve the spicy Thai basil chicken hot over cooked rice.

Enjoy your flavorful and spicy Thai Basil Chicken! Adjust the level of spiciness according to your preference by adding more or fewer Thai bird's eye chilies.

Eggplant Parmesan

Ingredients:

- 2 large eggplants
- Salt
- 2 cups breadcrumbs (you can use Italian seasoned breadcrumbs or plain breadcrumbs mixed with Italian seasoning)
- 1 cup grated Parmesan cheese
- 3 large eggs, beaten
- 2 cups marinara sauce (homemade or store-bought)
- 2 cups shredded mozzarella cheese
- Fresh basil leaves, chopped (optional, for garnish)
- Olive oil, for frying

Instructions:

1. Prepare the Eggplant:
    - Peel the eggplants (optional) and slice them into 1/4-inch thick rounds.
    - Place the eggplant slices in a colander and sprinkle them with salt. Let them sit for about 30 minutes to release excess moisture. Rinse the salt off the eggplant slices and pat them dry with paper towels.
2. Bread and Fry the Eggplant:
    - In a shallow dish, mix together breadcrumbs and grated Parmesan cheese.
    - Dip each eggplant slice into the beaten eggs, then coat it with the breadcrumb mixture, pressing gently to adhere.
    - Heat olive oil in a large skillet over medium heat. Fry the breaded eggplant slices in batches until golden brown on both sides, about 2-3 minutes per side. Transfer the fried eggplant slices to a paper towel-lined plate to drain excess oil.
3. Assemble the Dish:
    - Preheat the oven to 375°F (190°C).
    - Spread a thin layer of marinara sauce on the bottom of a baking dish.
    - Arrange a layer of fried eggplant slices over the marinara sauce.
    - Spoon more marinara sauce over the eggplant slices, then sprinkle with shredded mozzarella cheese.
    - Repeat the layers until all the eggplant slices are used, finishing with a layer of marinara sauce and shredded mozzarella cheese on top.
4. Bake:
    - Cover the baking dish with aluminum foil and bake in the preheated oven for 25-30 minutes, or until the cheese is melted and bubbly.
    - Remove the foil and bake for an additional 5-10 minutes, or until the cheese is golden brown.
5. Serve:
    - Let the Eggplant Parmesan cool for a few minutes before serving.
    - Garnish with chopped fresh basil leaves, if desired.

- Serve hot and enjoy!

Eggplant Parmesan pairs wonderfully with a side of pasta or a fresh green salad. It's a comforting and satisfying dish that's perfect for any occasion!

Honey Garlic Glazed Salmon

Ingredients:

- 4 salmon fillets, skin-on or skinless
- Salt and black pepper, to taste
- 2 tablespoons olive oil
- 4 cloves garlic, minced
- 1/4 cup honey
- 2 tablespoons soy sauce
- 1 tablespoon lemon juice
- 1 tablespoon water
- Optional: Sesame seeds and chopped green onions for garnish

Instructions:

1. Prepare the Salmon:
    - Pat the salmon fillets dry with paper towels. Season both sides of the salmon with salt and black pepper to taste.
2. Make the Honey Garlic Glaze:
    - In a small bowl, whisk together minced garlic, honey, soy sauce, lemon juice, and water until well combined. Set aside.
3. Cook the Salmon:
    - Heat olive oil in a large skillet over medium-high heat.
    - Once the oil is hot, add the salmon fillets to the skillet, skin-side down if using skin-on fillets. Cook for 3-4 minutes without moving, allowing the skin to crisp up (if applicable).
    - Flip the salmon fillets over and cook for an additional 3-4 minutes, or until the salmon is cooked to your desired doneness and easily flakes with a fork.
    - If the fillets are thick, you may need to cover the skillet with a lid or foil to help them cook through.
4. Add the Glaze:
    - Reduce the heat to medium-low. Pour the honey garlic glaze over the salmon fillets in the skillet.
    - Allow the glaze to simmer for 1-2 minutes, spooning it over the salmon occasionally, until it thickens slightly and coats the salmon nicely.
5. Serve:
    - Once the salmon is glazed and cooked through, remove the skillet from the heat.

- Transfer the salmon fillets to serving plates. Spoon any remaining glaze from the skillet over the salmon.
- Garnish with sesame seeds and chopped green onions, if desired.

6. Enjoy! Serve the Honey Garlic Glazed Salmon hot, accompanied by your favorite sides such as steamed vegetables, rice, or quinoa. The combination of sweet and savory flavors makes this dish a favorite for seafood lovers!

Mushroom Risotto Stuffed Bell Peppers

Ingredients:

- 4 large bell peppers (any color), halved and seeds removed
- 1 cup Arborio rice
- 4 cups vegetable or chicken broth
- 2 tablespoons olive oil
- 1 onion, finely chopped
- 2 cloves garlic, minced
- 8 oz (225g) mushrooms, sliced (such as cremini or button mushrooms)
- 1/2 cup dry white wine (optional)
- 1/2 cup grated Parmesan cheese
- Salt and pepper, to taste
- Fresh parsley, chopped, for garnish

Instructions:

1. Preheat the Oven:
    - Preheat your oven to 375°F (190°C). Prepare a baking dish large enough to hold all the bell pepper halves.
2. Prepare the Bell Peppers:
    - Cut the bell peppers in half lengthwise and remove the seeds and membranes. Place the pepper halves cut-side up in the baking dish.
3. Prepare the Risotto:
    - In a medium saucepan, heat the vegetable or chicken broth over medium heat until it simmers. Reduce the heat to low to keep it warm.
    - In a large skillet or pot, heat olive oil over medium heat. Add the chopped onion and cook until softened, about 3-4 minutes.
    - Add the minced garlic and sliced mushrooms to the skillet. Cook, stirring occasionally, until the mushrooms are golden brown and softened, about 5-6 minutes.
    - Stir in the Arborio rice and cook for 1-2 minutes, stirring constantly, until the rice is coated with the oil and slightly translucent.
    - If using, pour in the white wine and cook, stirring frequently, until the wine has evaporated.
    - Begin adding the warm broth to the skillet, one ladleful at a time, stirring frequently and allowing the liquid to absorb before adding more. Continue this process until the rice is creamy and cooked al dente, about 20-25 minutes.

4. Finish the Risotto:
    - Once the risotto is cooked to your desired consistency, stir in the grated Parmesan cheese. Season with salt and pepper to taste.
5. Stuff the Bell Peppers:
    - Fill each bell pepper half with the prepared mushroom risotto, pressing it down gently to fill the cavity.
6. Bake:
    - Place the stuffed bell peppers in the preheated oven and bake for 25-30 minutes, or until the peppers are tender and slightly charred on the edges.
7. Serve:
    - Remove the stuffed bell peppers from the oven and let them cool for a few minutes.
    - Garnish with chopped fresh parsley before serving.

These Mushroom Risotto Stuffed Bell Peppers make a delicious and elegant meal, perfect for a special dinner or a vegetarian main course option. Enjoy!

Lemon Herb Grilled Lamb Chops

Ingredients:

- 8 lamb chops (about 1 1/2 inches thick)
- 1/4 cup olive oil
- 3 tablespoons fresh lemon juice
- Zest of 1 lemon
- 3 cloves garlic, minced
- 2 tablespoons fresh herbs (such as rosemary, thyme, and oregano), finely chopped
- 1 teaspoon dried oregano
- Salt and black pepper, to taste

Instructions:

1. Marinate the Lamb Chops:
    - In a shallow dish or large resealable plastic bag, combine olive oil, fresh lemon juice, lemon zest, minced garlic, chopped fresh herbs, dried oregano, salt, and black pepper. Mix well to combine.
    - Add the lamb chops to the marinade, ensuring they are evenly coated. Cover the dish or seal the bag and marinate in the refrigerator for at least 2 hours, or preferably overnight, to allow the flavors to meld and the meat to tenderize.
2. Preheat the Grill:
    - Preheat your grill to medium-high heat (about 400°F to 450°F or 200°C to 230°C). Make sure the grill grates are clean and lightly oiled to prevent sticking.
3. Grill the Lamb Chops:
    - Remove the lamb chops from the marinade and discard any excess marinade.
    - Place the lamb chops on the preheated grill. Grill for about 4-5 minutes on each side for medium-rare, or adjust the cooking time according to your desired level of doneness.
    - Use a meat thermometer to check the internal temperature of the lamb chops. For medium-rare, the temperature should read around 145°F (63°C).
4. Rest and Serve:

- Once the lamb chops are cooked to your liking, transfer them to a plate or cutting board and let them rest for a few minutes. This allows the juices to redistribute throughout the meat.
- Serve the grilled lamb chops hot, garnished with fresh herbs and lemon wedges if desired.

These Lemon Herb Grilled Lamb Chops are delicious served with a side of roasted vegetables, couscous, or a fresh salad. Enjoy the tender, flavorful meat infused with zesty lemon and aromatic herbs!

Cajun Shrimp and Sausage Skillet

Ingredients:

- 1 pound large shrimp, peeled and deveined
- 12 oz (about 4 links) Andouille sausage, sliced into rounds
- 1 tablespoon Cajun seasoning (adjust to taste)
- 2 tablespoons olive oil
- 1 onion, diced
- 1 bell pepper, diced (any color)
- 3 cloves garlic, minced
- 1 can (14.5 oz) diced tomatoes, drained
- 1 cup chicken broth
- Salt and pepper, to taste
- Cooked rice, for serving
- Fresh parsley, chopped, for garnish (optional)

Instructions:

1. Season the Shrimp and Sausage:
    - In a bowl, toss the peeled and deveined shrimp and sliced Andouille sausage with Cajun seasoning until evenly coated. Set aside.
2. Sauté the Sausage and Vegetables:
    - Heat olive oil in a large skillet over medium-high heat. Add the sliced Andouille sausage to the skillet and cook until browned, about 3-4 minutes per side. Remove the sausage from the skillet and set aside.
    - In the same skillet, add diced onion and bell pepper. Sauté until softened, about 3-4 minutes.
    - Add minced garlic to the skillet and cook for an additional 1 minute, stirring constantly.
3. Cook the Shrimp:
    - Return the cooked Andouille sausage to the skillet with the vegetables.
    - Add the seasoned shrimp to the skillet and cook until pink and opaque, about 2-3 minutes per side.
4. Add Tomatoes and Broth:
    - Once the shrimp is cooked, add the drained diced tomatoes to the skillet, stirring to combine.
    - Pour in the chicken broth and stir well. Allow the mixture to come to a simmer.
5. Simmer:

- Reduce the heat to medium-low and let the skillet simmer for 5-7 minutes, allowing the flavors to meld and the sauce to thicken slightly.
- Season with salt and pepper to taste.

6. Serve:
    - Serve the Cajun shrimp and sausage mixture hot over cooked rice.
    - Garnish with chopped fresh parsley, if desired.

This Cajun Shrimp and Sausage Skillet is bursting with flavor and can be customized with additional Cajun seasoning for extra heat. It's a satisfying and comforting dish that's sure to become a favorite!

Chicken and Spinach Quesadillas

Ingredients:

- 2 cups cooked chicken breast, shredded or diced
- 2 cups fresh spinach leaves, chopped
- 1 cup shredded cheese (such as cheddar, Monterey Jack, or a Mexican cheese blend)
- 1/2 cup diced onion
- 1/2 cup diced bell pepper (any color)
- 1 teaspoon ground cumin
- 1 teaspoon chili powder
- Salt and pepper, to taste
- 4 large flour tortillas
- Olive oil or cooking spray, for cooking
- Sour cream, salsa, and guacamole, for serving (optional)

Instructions:

1. Prepare the Filling:
    - In a large mixing bowl, combine the cooked chicken breast, chopped spinach leaves, shredded cheese, diced onion, diced bell pepper, ground cumin, chili powder, salt, and pepper. Mix well to combine.
2. Assemble the Quesadillas:
    - Lay out one flour tortilla on a flat surface. Spread a generous portion of the chicken and spinach mixture evenly over half of the tortilla, leaving a border around the edges.
    - Fold the other half of the tortilla over the filling to create a half-moon shape.
3. Cook the Quesadillas:
    - Heat a large skillet or griddle over medium heat. Lightly brush the surface with olive oil or coat it with cooking spray.
    - Place the assembled quesadilla in the skillet and cook for 2-3 minutes on each side, or until golden brown and crispy, and the cheese is melted.
    - Repeat the process with the remaining tortillas and filling.
4. Serve:
    - Once cooked, transfer the quesadillas to a cutting board and let them cool for a minute before slicing them into wedges.
    - Serve the chicken and spinach quesadillas hot, accompanied by sour cream, salsa, and guacamole for dipping, if desired.

These chicken and spinach quesadillas are versatile, and you can customize them by adding other ingredients like sliced mushrooms, black beans, or corn. They're a crowd-pleaser and perfect for a quick and satisfying meal!

Beef Wellington with Red Wine Sauce

Ingredients for Beef Wellington:

- 4 beef fillet steaks (about 6 oz each), preferably center-cut and of equal thickness
- Salt and black pepper, to taste
- 2 tablespoons olive oil
- 1 tablespoon Dijon mustard
- 8 slices prosciutto or Parma ham
- 1 package (17.5 oz) puff pastry, thawed if frozen
- 1 egg, beaten (for egg wash)

For the Mushroom Duxelles:

- 1 tablespoon olive oil
- 2 shallots, finely chopped
- 2 cloves garlic, minced
- 12 oz mushrooms (such as button or cremini), finely chopped
- 1 tablespoon fresh thyme leaves
- Salt and black pepper, to taste

For the Red Wine Sauce:

- 1 tablespoon olive oil
- 1 shallot, finely chopped
- 1 cup red wine
- 1 cup beef broth
- 2 tablespoons unsalted butter, cold
- Salt and black pepper, to taste

Instructions:

1. Prepare the Beef Fillets:
    - Season the beef fillet steaks generously with salt and black pepper on both sides.
    - Heat olive oil in a large skillet over high heat. Sear the beef fillets for about 1-2 minutes on each side until browned. Remove from heat and let them cool slightly.
2. Prepare the Mushroom Duxelles:
    - In the same skillet, heat olive oil over medium heat. Add chopped shallots and garlic, and cook until softened, about 2-3 minutes.

- Add finely chopped mushrooms and thyme leaves to the skillet. Cook, stirring occasionally, until the mushrooms release their moisture and the mixture becomes dry, about 10-12 minutes. Season with salt and black pepper to taste. Remove from heat and let it cool.

3. Assemble the Beef Wellington:
    - Preheat the oven to 400°F (200°C).
    - Brush each seared beef fillet with Dijon mustard.
    - Place 2 slices of prosciutto or Parma ham on a clean surface, slightly overlapping. Spread a layer of mushroom duxelles over the prosciutto.
    - Place the beef fillet on top of the mushroom duxelles. Carefully roll the prosciutto and mushroom mixture around the beef fillet to form a tight bundle. Repeat with the remaining fillets.
    - Roll out the puff pastry on a lightly floured surface. Cut the pastry into squares large enough to enclose each beef bundle. Place each beef bundle in the center of a pastry square.
    - Fold the pastry over the beef bundle, sealing the edges with a little beaten egg. Trim any excess pastry if necessary. Place the wrapped beef Wellingtons seam-side down on a baking sheet lined with parchment paper.
    - Brush the tops of the pastry with beaten egg for a golden finish.
4. Bake the Beef Wellington:
    - Bake in the preheated oven for 20-25 minutes, or until the pastry is golden brown and crispy, and the beef reaches your desired level of doneness (medium-rare is recommended for best flavor).
5. Make the Red Wine Sauce:
    - While the beef Wellingtons are baking, prepare the red wine sauce. In a saucepan, heat olive oil over medium heat. Add finely chopped shallot and cook until softened, about 2-3 minutes.
    - Pour in the red wine and beef broth. Bring the mixture to a simmer and cook until reduced by half, stirring occasionally, about 15-20 minutes.
    - Remove the saucepan from heat and whisk in cold butter until melted and incorporated into the sauce. Season with salt and black pepper to taste.
6. Serve:
    - Once the beef Wellingtons are done, let them rest for a few minutes before slicing. Serve the sliced beef Wellingtons with the red wine sauce on the side.

Beef Wellington with Red Wine Sauce is a gourmet delight that's sure to impress your guests. Enjoy this decadent dish for a special dinner occasion!

Greek Lemon Chicken with Orzo

Ingredients:

- 4 boneless, skinless chicken breasts
- Salt and black pepper, to taste
- 2 tablespoons olive oil
- 4 cloves garlic, minced
- 1 teaspoon dried oregano
- 1 teaspoon dried thyme
- 1 teaspoon dried rosemary
- Zest and juice of 2 lemons
- 1 cup chicken broth
- 1 cup cherry tomatoes, halved
- 1 cup baby spinach leaves
- 1 cup uncooked orzo pasta
- Crumbled feta cheese, for serving (optional)
- Chopped fresh parsley, for garnish

Instructions:

1. Season and Sear the Chicken:
    - Season the chicken breasts with salt and black pepper on both sides.
    - Heat olive oil in a large skillet over medium-high heat. Add the chicken breasts to the skillet and cook for 4-5 minutes on each side until golden brown and cooked through. Remove the chicken from the skillet and set aside.
2. Prepare the Lemon Herb Sauce:
    - In the same skillet, reduce the heat to medium. Add minced garlic, dried oregano, dried thyme, and dried rosemary. Cook for about 1 minute until fragrant.
    - Stir in the lemon zest and lemon juice, scraping up any browned bits from the bottom of the skillet.
    - Pour in the chicken broth and bring the mixture to a simmer. Let it simmer for 2-3 minutes to allow the flavors to meld.
3. Cook the Orzo:
    - Meanwhile, cook the orzo pasta according to the package instructions in a separate pot of boiling salted water until al dente. Drain and set aside.
4. Add the Chicken and Vegetables:

- Return the cooked chicken breasts to the skillet with the lemon herb sauce. Add halved cherry tomatoes and baby spinach leaves to the skillet, stirring to combine. Let the mixture simmer for an additional 2-3 minutes until the spinach wilts and the tomatoes soften slightly.

5. Serve:
    - To serve, place a portion of cooked orzo on each plate. Top with a chicken breast and spoon the lemon herb sauce, tomatoes, and spinach over the chicken.
    - Garnish with crumbled feta cheese (if using) and chopped fresh parsley.
    - Serve the Greek Lemon Chicken with Orzo hot and enjoy!

This Greek-inspired dish is bursting with fresh flavors and makes a satisfying meal for any occasion. Serve it with a side of crusty bread or a Greek salad for a complete and delicious meal.

Baked Halibut with Herbed Butter

Ingredients:

- 4 halibut fillets (about 6 oz each)
- Salt and black pepper, to taste
- 2 tablespoons olive oil
- 1/4 cup unsalted butter, softened
- 2 cloves garlic, minced
- 1 tablespoon fresh lemon juice
- 1 tablespoon chopped fresh parsley
- 1 tablespoon chopped fresh dill
- 1 tablespoon chopped fresh chives
- 1 teaspoon lemon zest

Instructions:

1. Preheat the Oven:
   - Preheat your oven to 375°F (190°C).
2. Prepare the Herbed Butter:
   - In a small bowl, combine the softened butter, minced garlic, fresh lemon juice, chopped parsley, chopped dill, chopped chives, and lemon zest. Mix until well combined. Season with salt and black pepper to taste.
3. Prepare the Halibut:
   - Pat the halibut fillets dry with paper towels. Season both sides of the halibut fillets with salt and black pepper.
   - Place the seasoned halibut fillets in a baking dish lightly greased with olive oil, making sure they are not overcrowded.
4. Top with Herbed Butter:
   - Spread a generous portion of the herbed butter over the top of each halibut fillet, covering them evenly.
5. Bake the Halibut:
   - Transfer the baking dish to the preheated oven and bake for 12-15 minutes, or until the halibut is cooked through and flakes easily with a fork.
6. Serve:
   - Once the halibut is cooked, remove it from the oven and let it rest for a few minutes.
   - Serve the baked halibut fillets hot, garnished with additional chopped fresh herbs and lemon wedges if desired.

This Baked Halibut with Herbed Butter is a simple yet elegant dish that's perfect for a special dinner or a weeknight meal. The flavorful herbed butter adds richness and depth to the delicate halibut fillets, creating a truly delicious dining experience. Enjoy!

Stuffed Portobello Mushrooms

Ingredients:

- 4 large Portobello mushrooms, stems removed
- 2 tablespoons olive oil
- 2 cloves garlic, minced
- 1 small onion, finely chopped
- 1 cup baby spinach, chopped
- 1/2 cup sun-dried tomatoes, chopped
- 1/2 cup breadcrumbs (plain or seasoned)
- 1/2 cup grated Parmesan cheese
- Salt and black pepper, to taste
- 1/4 cup chopped fresh parsley, for garnish

Instructions:

1. Preheat the Oven:
    - Preheat your oven to 375°F (190°C).
2. Prepare the Portobello Mushrooms:
    - Clean the Portobello mushrooms by wiping them gently with a damp cloth or paper towel. Remove the stems and scoop out the gills using a spoon to create a hollow cavity in each mushroom cap.
3. Prepare the Filling:
    - Heat olive oil in a skillet over medium heat. Add minced garlic and chopped onion, and sauté until softened, about 2-3 minutes.
    - Add chopped baby spinach and sun-dried tomatoes to the skillet. Cook for an additional 2-3 minutes until the spinach wilts.
    - Remove the skillet from heat and stir in breadcrumbs and grated Parmesan cheese until well combined. Season with salt and black pepper to taste.
4. Stuff the Mushrooms:
    - Place the Portobello mushroom caps on a baking sheet lined with parchment paper or aluminum foil.
    - Divide the filling mixture evenly among the mushroom caps, pressing it down gently to pack it into the cavities.
5. Bake:
    - Transfer the baking sheet to the preheated oven and bake for 20-25 minutes, or until the mushrooms are tender and the filling is golden brown and crispy.

6. Serve:
    - Once baked, remove the stuffed Portobello mushrooms from the oven and let them cool for a few minutes.
    - Garnish with chopped fresh parsley before serving.

These Stuffed Portobello Mushrooms are flavorful, hearty, and versatile. They can be served as an appetizer, a side dish, or even as a main course paired with a salad or some crusty bread. Enjoy!

Turkey Meatballs with Marinara Sauce

Ingredients for Turkey Meatballs:

- 1 pound ground turkey (preferably lean)
- 1/2 cup breadcrumbs (plain or Italian seasoned)
- 1/4 cup grated Parmesan cheese
- 1 egg
- 2 cloves garlic, minced
- 2 tablespoons chopped fresh parsley
- 1 teaspoon dried oregano
- 1/2 teaspoon salt
- 1/4 teaspoon black pepper
- Olive oil, for frying

Ingredients for Marinara Sauce:

- 1 tablespoon olive oil
- 1 small onion, finely chopped
- 2 cloves garlic, minced
- 1 can (28 oz) crushed tomatoes
- 1 teaspoon dried oregano
- 1 teaspoon dried basil
- 1/2 teaspoon dried thyme
- Salt and black pepper, to taste
- Pinch of sugar (optional, to balance acidity)

Instructions:

1. Prepare the Turkey Meatballs:
    - In a large mixing bowl, combine ground turkey, breadcrumbs, grated Parmesan cheese, egg, minced garlic, chopped parsley, dried oregano, salt, and black pepper. Mix until well combined.
    - Shape the mixture into meatballs, about 1 to 1.5 inches in diameter.
2. Cook the Turkey Meatballs:
    - Heat olive oil in a large skillet over medium heat. Add the turkey meatballs in batches, making sure not to overcrowd the pan. Cook for about 5-6 minutes, turning occasionally, until browned on all sides and cooked through. Transfer the cooked meatballs to a plate and set aside.
3. Make the Marinara Sauce:

- In the same skillet, add another tablespoon of olive oil if needed. Add finely chopped onion and cook until softened, about 3-4 minutes. Add minced garlic and cook for an additional minute until fragrant.
- Pour in the crushed tomatoes and stir to combine. Add dried oregano, dried basil, dried thyme, salt, black pepper, and a pinch of sugar if desired (to balance the acidity of the tomatoes).
- Bring the sauce to a simmer and let it cook for about 10-15 minutes, stirring occasionally, until slightly thickened.

4. Finish Cooking the Meatballs:
    - Return the cooked turkey meatballs to the skillet with the marinara sauce. Spoon some sauce over the meatballs.
    - Simmer the meatballs in the sauce for an additional 5-10 minutes to allow the flavors to meld and the meatballs to absorb some of the sauce.
5. Serve:
    - Once the meatballs are heated through and the sauce is flavorful, remove the skillet from heat.
    - Serve the turkey meatballs with marinara sauce hot, garnished with chopped fresh parsley or grated Parmesan cheese if desired.

These turkey meatballs with marinara sauce are delicious served over cooked pasta or zucchini noodles, or as a filling for sandwiches or subs. Enjoy this lighter and healthier twist on a classic comfort food!

Pan-Seared Scallops with Brown Butter Sauce

Ingredients:

- 1 pound fresh sea scallops, patted dry
- Salt and black pepper, to taste
- 2 tablespoons olive oil or clarified butter (ghee)

For the Brown Butter Sauce:

- 4 tablespoons unsalted butter
- 2 cloves garlic, minced
- 2 tablespoons fresh lemon juice
- 1 tablespoon chopped fresh parsley
- Salt and black pepper, to taste

Instructions:

1. Prepare the Scallops:
    - Pat the scallops dry with paper towels to remove any excess moisture. Season both sides of the scallops with salt and black pepper.
2. Heat the Pan:
    - Heat olive oil or clarified butter in a large skillet over medium-high heat until hot but not smoking. It's important for the skillet to be hot to achieve a good sear on the scallops.
3. Sear the Scallops:
    - Carefully add the scallops to the hot skillet, making sure they are not overcrowded. Leave space between each scallop to ensure even cooking.
    - Cook the scallops without moving them for about 2-3 minutes on each side, or until they develop a golden brown crust. Avoid overcrowding the pan to prevent steaming the scallops instead of searing them.
4. Make the Brown Butter Sauce:
    - While the scallops are cooking, prepare the brown butter sauce. In a separate small saucepan, melt the unsalted butter over medium heat.
    - Once the butter has melted, continue cooking, swirling the pan occasionally, until the butter turns golden brown and develops a nutty aroma, about 3-5 minutes. Be careful not to let the butter burn.
    - Add minced garlic to the brown butter and cook for an additional 1-2 minutes until fragrant.

- Remove the saucepan from heat and stir in fresh lemon juice and chopped fresh parsley. Season with salt and black pepper to taste.

5. Serve:
    - Once the scallops are cooked to your liking and have developed a nice sear on both sides, transfer them to a serving platter or individual plates.
    - Spoon the brown butter sauce over the scallops, making sure to distribute the garlic and parsley evenly.
    - Serve the pan-seared scallops with brown butter sauce immediately, garnished with additional fresh parsley or lemon wedges if desired.

These pan-seared scallops with brown butter sauce are best enjoyed hot and fresh. Serve them as an appetizer or as a main course paired with your favorite side dishes for a luxurious and flavorful meal!